Rolling Stock

HUBERT MOORE

Rolling Stock

ENITHARMON PRESS 1991

First published in 1991
by the Enitharmon Press
40 Rushes Road
Petersfield
Hampshire GU32 3BW

ISBN 1 870612 51 5

Set in 10pt Ehrhardt by Bryan Williamson, Darwen
and printed by
Antony Rowe Limited, Chippenham, Wiltshire

This edition is limited to 500 copies

ACKNOWLEDGEMENTS

Acknowledgements are due to the editors of the following:

Argo, Iron, London Review of Books, Other Poetry, Oxford Magazine, Prospice, The Printer's Devil, South West Review

Contents

Crossing the Church

Some seem born to it. They could cross
the gleaming track from the nave to the altar
blindfold.

Look, no hands even. Now they're squaring
their shoulders eastwards, gravely inclining
their heads;

and now they're over, strolling off amidst pews,
leaving one at least of us standing
helpless

as ever to help the children we were,
who anyway couldn't be helped,
born

trespassers, laying our ears
to the cold steel of the track, hearing
the rail

singing the song that we hoped for,
five miles off, centuries still
for us,

knees bare on the flinty stone,
heads where the wheels would be rolling –
then scrambling safely across.

Daughter

It's dark still as we drive five
simple miles to catch her train.
No one else on the roads: we dazzle
nothing, nothing dazzles us. We let
our headlights nose in the hedges
a hundred yards ahead. The moon,
in open sky to our left, lays
cottages flat in their own
front gardens, burns trees black
on the white water of orchards,
and angles in undipped, unblinking
on my beloved passenger,
awake now, going calmly to work.

Driving home I find I'm thinking
who's this behind me somewhere
to my right not quite following
– there's no light in the mirror –
yet not so road-hogging or rash
to overtake me?

Both Indias

(for Alison and Stephen)

'Look and to morrow late, tell mee
Whether both the India's of Spice and Myne
Be where thou leftst them...'   (Donne)

Well, not Spice exactly, but
an India of parchedness for each other,
for Alison in Kent,
for Steve somewhere in Essex –
and us thinking the Thames Estuary
lay untunnelled between you.

From flat to flat to your first
property, in West Yorkshire:
deep beneath you, riddled
with workings, worked through to the bone,
this first – now obsolete –
ground of yours: an India of Myne.

Above, at the hole in the hillside,
cranes come dangling, and the gaunt
lop-sided A-shape is dismantled.
Stand at your kitchen window,
watch it happening: the skyline
clearing, mine becoming ours.

The Night Attendant

At home, on winter nights
when no one else is crossing
(Southampton – Le Havre or Cherbourg,
Portsmouth – St Malo), he waits

grimly indulgent, alone
in his cabin, till she's way
off shore, past The Needles,
past the red eyes of the buoys,

then tip-toes in, can hear
through the steady jar of the engines
there are passengers sleeping –
this one under the wing

of her shoulder, hands clasped
to her collar-bone, face
abandoned. He closes her book;
turns the bedside light off; even

gives her the same sleep twice –
sits at his desk from midnight
to 1 am, adjusts his watch, sits
at his desk from midnight to 1 am.

At dawn he draws back the curtains.
Morning after morning he shows her
her first sight of land. Look,
she can see houses quite clearly.

His Move

Emptying their flat: we stuff
my van for a day then go, some
quivering stiff-necked pot-plant
she's rejected, beside me
in the passenger-seat, pampered
with cricket-gear. In front,
on the floor, a dog's body of books
next to the gear-lever. Last things
on the dashboard: keys, cheque-book,
a statement of their joint account.

We drive a hundred yards low-geared,
back doors open, up the road
and across it. Behind the blank
wall of their dining-table he
walks keeping their bed in place.
It's dark as we make the journey.

Cars coming towards us primly
avert their gaze; those overtaking
flip up their eyes as they pass
the man at the edge of my wing-
mirror, arms lifted, saving
something from falling, his face
on fire in the tail-light, then,
as we come to his turning, glinting
I'm turning, I'm turning, I'm turning.

Bowls Players

Two or three go

this way each winter. Not actually
buried here, though they used to be,
under the lime-trees, over the wall
from the broad slope of the Pay-
and-Leave Recreation Ground Carpark,
so well placed for the Bowls players.

Not five minutes up from their cars,
the Bowling Green is the first flat
earth you come to, hedged, private;
walking past you hear the same music
all summer: the clocking of woods,
the gentle exclaiming of voices.

When the light goes, you can see them
wheeling down off the edge of the world,
balanced on end, upright – to the lone
Jack in the Carpark they might be
totally still – till their rolling slows
and they tip sideways into precisely

what they came in.

Ringers

Shoulder-high that parapet must be
up in the bell-tower. Now you see,

nose first (bell-pulling hands for noses),
whole shirt-sleeved upper bodies

leap for the scraps we throw them;
now they're immersed in the stream

of the huge underwater gonging
they make of their Sunday ringing.

The ringers have finished of course,
when we lower-body worshippers

are only beginning: off they slip
as the opening prayers come up,

flickering across bright areas
of open church, from the tower staircase

to some private creek – dark, see-through –
that the South Entry leads to.

Son

The storm last night must have come
careering down this lane: the swept
hair of the hedges, leaves left
in the mould of the rain's rippling stroke.

Coming down off the fields you tread
in their washed silvery topsoil,
the soft silt of a stream-bed
almost uncreased, unslept in.

No wonder we lay awake:
hearing the flicked curtain of rain
kick-start into the night,
then flatten itself on our window;

listening through it, like listening
for light, for the first
lovely tentative gurgle
up the garden-path of our son's

motor-bike. This morning
every hollow in town looks blandly up
as if it had been its own
pond since Domesday at least.

Seven am November

Dawn, you could say. Webs of it
furring the streetlamps, strung
from hedge to hedge of the lane,
from the bridge of his nose
to his temples. Dawn all day

for the blind man coming,
nose down over his stick,
elbows jutted for obstacles,
fut-fut-futting through early
morning mist on the white

motor-bike of his blindness.
The loom of me moves aside,
dodges out of his aura: into
bright day – my day, planned
already, her day, his day

whom I should by now be calling
back from his runaway dreams –
upstairs, mumbling his curses
at motorists, riding to work
before he rides to work, day

all his dawn.

Clay

Five days from a visit to Dublin,
five years after one, fields –
carved up from the clay-face,
ploughed now it's November –

gleam in the grainy daylight,
seamless as water, catchy
as cut glass: stockinged
legs and legs and legs

of Dublin girl-secretaries
flickering across wet pavements
through head-light and tail-light
(their carefully lowered gaze),

through the mesh
of shop-light and street-light and light
drifting up through the fingers
of basement kitchens

and rain steadily falling
its last few feet onto Ireland,
due, so the forecast says,
to spread across England tomorrow,

shining the face of the fields there,
making the mirrors imagine
what next week I gazed at,
years ago will be revisiting.

Ockham's Razor

('Entities ought not to be multiplied except of necessity')

Ockham's razor is visible

at certain dawns and dusks
and on vague November afternoons

when tears form at the lit
windows of buildings, and streetlamps
tremble at the brink of the eyes.

Even when no one can see it,
it's there of course, angling in
on the beard's latest upshoots –
wheatfield, bristle of daffodils;

always there, unsheathed,
hovering over phenomena:
the rusty hinge of a goose-call
that woke me this morning
creaking with likenesses;

or, yellow as lemons, the last
few unreachable ones
on the apple-tree, the arms
of the reacher upraised
as if pleading the case
with William of Ockham himself

for licence, poetic licence.

Shade

Bedded with sleepers once, long since
leaf-moulded, the grand carriageway
tunnelling up through the trees
from the great house
to where the great gates were,

now an almost subterranean
public footpath, up which
my father walked halfway, slowly,
savouring the eeriness.
A connoisseur of shade,

its furred-up stillnesses, the close
grain of its silence: thick of the air
you could stand up a birch-tree in
or an elderly man,
tall, squaring his shoulders

at the sudden, oil-less wheels
of a woodpecker passing.
Unless that's the cry shades make
when, halfway up,
someone looks back at them.

For Jackie

Weeks it seems since the phone-call
on Sunday night – Keith
not joking 'Rembrandt here' for once,
but saying you were ill in hospital.

You must be counting, drip
by gathering drip, the days, the nights,
since that first morning you woke
knowing the tests had been positive –

as we've been counting, in Kent,
the days since the snow started:
farmland quite near us they showed on TV,
every feature sheeted.

Get well again, Jackie. Be
the green in the damp bruised grass
that, when the thaw comes, flares
like light in the black of a Rembrandt.

Maundy Thursday

Weeks after winter prodigal
snow came back in the early hours
and lies where it fell or leans
against wherever it happens
to have drifted. Bound and gagged
we try walking out together,

and the graveyard this morning
is a picture by one of the Brueghels:
all graves gone and the headstones
diving delightedly each at its
angle anyhow into the snow,
heels up, legs tapering splashless,

or else shot streamlined
into the air, their bodies rigid
with what they hold at the tips
of their fingers: a thin half-moon
of silver coined for the day, something
for nothing, like what used to be dole.

Rolling Stock

Cross the canal, drop bicycles in the hedge,
perch on the railwaymen's stile. Eyes
at fire-box level, eyes on fire,
watch the tank-engines cannoning
coal-trucks, brick-trucks, empty carriages
into their lines; craning forwards, dare them
to do their tricks for us – grind brakes,
wheeze steam suddenly, whistle
with nothing to whistle at, turn sixpences
into shillings as they grate past on our line.

Come home, the three of us, to various
named characters: Grandpa – the billiards Grandpa –
starting from nothing, from a difficult in-
off-white, then a cannon, then an easy
cannon to come; Grandpa Holmes whistling
at meal-times; Crowe, married to Muriel,
twice his size; and Uncle Percy, who,
one Harvest Festival Service, chose for himself
from the pile on the window-ledge an apple,
and cracked it open while we froze in prayer.

Hear such loose-linking 1940s incidents
shake couplings, whistle, then drag off
into the distance. Hear the bouncing drop
of a signal, points scuttling over, a tank-
engine like some tin-pot deity
blasting off, then, wheels gently insisting,
throbbing along our line, three rigid
carriages glide by. See, from the top rung
of our perch in the marshalling-yard, craning
towards us, ourselves, ourselves, ourselves.

The Curve of Forgetting

The main line of the graph
is continuous: it represents
the memory progressing, station
by station, across a dense
landscape of facts. By Day Six
of the process, for instance,
80% has been memorised.

The line sets out from London –
Liverpool Street, I suppose – north-east
to Ipswich or Felixstowe,
via Brentwood, Chelmsford, Colchester,
from each of which there rises
another line, dotted, a ghost
of backward-floating smoke.

This is the curve of forgetting,
setting off up country,
up a ladder of prostrate sleepers,
pine after pine of them gradually
narrowing, gradually veering
west as a scream comes by,
then boys unmanned at a crossing.

Disused, uneconomical,
brambled over now, the dots
on the graph are merely
hypothetical points where what's
matter of course, too trivial
not to forget, meets
what's too terrible to remember.

The Rains

A steady downpour peppering
the water: page after page
it prints, from nine am to five,
every finger in action touch-
typing the pond Dear Madam,
We are sorry...we sincerely
hope...we trust...we remain.

At last it finishes and they
click off on stilts from pool
to pool of pure unspotted lamp-
light. Back in their offices,
their zipped-up typewriters
slump forward at their desks,
mackintosh tops gleaming.

Meanwhile another rain: gathered
over the pond, all evening
willow-branches, leaf-trough
by leaf-trough, brim and spill,
pitting the calm new water.
Sometimes Dear Madam finds
she weeps when she's not weeping.

The Take-Away

As the crow flies
or the wind carries cooking-smells,
there's only an untarred lane –
its lakes, its bricky foothills –
between us: between our front entrance
and the back way into the Indian.

They're often out there
amidst their gleaming cars and the sleek
black sacks. Off-peak they'll button-hole me
about our dog coming scavenging
and what potion is advised, madam,
for the sick child of one of them.

They're ready though
on birthdays, paydays, when our ship
comes in – behind their veiled shopfront
lining the gangway. Pleased teeth glint
while, somewhere in the intimate
velvety dusk, our cartons are sealed.

Of course I travel
the posh way: cruise out down the High Street,
then, at a hint of monsoon weather
or change, come coasting home
the White Horse to starboard,
the take-away warm in my arms.

At the Port of London
everyone turns out to meet me –
my parents, his parents: asking no questions,
at the first peep under the coverlet
neither blushing nor blanching:
proud as Punch the Grandpas seem.

Old Dog

Past nearly everything now –
past bitches, past blustering up
at the saucy trapezing of squirrels
over his head, past even
pretending the postman's a thief
and the face at the window
is that of the smiling
mustachioed villain –

he sits up rigid
with interest and reads
the stories the dazed or the furious,
plotters with spectacles,
lean, with a sting in the tail,
or mere boring old buzzers,
trace on the window-pane
inches in front of his nose.

The bang of a body on glass
raises his ears, goes
through him, ripples the rod
of his tail. Even distant
droning stiffens him; and
at suddenly no such droning,
he tips his head for the sense of it,
reading between the lines.

Escape is his favourite genre –
or those stories in which
a character seeing before him
a picture of sky and a garden,
its green exactly in season,
its light the perfect light
of the day, flings himself into it,
at it, flat up against it.

For a Wedding Anniversary

She goes downstairs and the paper bag
she's left on the bed in the almost
empty room takes thirty years un-
crinkling. Letters printed across it –
the name and address of a woolshop –
creak apart to the latest shape
of her knitting: like the name carved
on the bark of the person she was
before marrying, its letters high
and wide and bodiless now, stretched
on the slow quake of her making.

By the Rhône-Rhine Canal

Fingers entwining, maybe
an arm thrown over the shoulders,
these huge-limbed chestnut-trees
make all day every day evening
along our stretch of canal.

Here nothing is moving. Water
brims in its water-trough; traffic
of time as of barges is obsolete.
All evening we sit, the two of us,
huge-limbed, weightless, by the canal,

as though, by opening sluices,
one or the other couldn't easily,
aimlessly drift down the map, through
widening gorges, to the river's mouth-
watering delta, les Bouches du Rhône,

or, merely locking off water,
float clean through Germany, further
and further northwards, high on the tide
of purer and purer Rhinewater,
up the sheer face of the map.

Huddersfield Narrow

Fed to the brim
then laid flat out in her cot,
she sees nothing
of the calm grazing animals
moving backwards past her
or the Pennines gathering:

enters Standedge Tunnel.
We peer through a grid up the last
few yards of reflection:
its criss-cross gleam
and the chiselled black ceiling
scuffed by what might be

upside-down footprints.
Not a cry from her cot
all evening: at twelve
we listen in through breathing
layers of hillside.
She'll be half way through by now –

no horse, no hands. Feet
flailing up at the blackness,
she stumbles along
under the fields' tap-roots,
this brightly painted barge
on her back.

Driving

We can go for miles like this:
no questions ever quite asked,
the windscreen-wipers' steady flick of the rope
and the rain's delicate ankles
skipping clear of it.

The Fire on the Mountain

We have our books, our drinks. All day
we lie in the thick shade of your vines.

We have the view beneath us: bleached roofs
of a village, a reservoir, then the huge

sand-dune of Spain. Behind, somewhere
up at the back of our heads

burns while we sleep our siestas,
burns while we talk through the night.

We wake long past the blare and jabber
of fire-engines: two ancient

sea-planes – Franco's planes they must be –
are still either droning down

over your vines or droning up
from the emptying pool beneath us:

old hands scooping water, cooling
the blistered face of the mountain.

But the fire's still there, still
at our backs, at the back of our heads

when we cross the plain for dinner,
try the local Parador, make sure

the Maestro is running as smoothly
as ever. Coming back in the dark,

we know where the mountain is
by the crown it wears while it's sleeping.

At Julio's

It might be our first fight
or our first operation.
White-suited, gauntleted, masked
– dressed to kill or cure –

we follow Julio's
bare back, straw-hatted head
up the crackle of oak leaves,
the winding path

into village after
mountainside village, hive
after hive simmering
with squat brown bodies,

a thick shoulder-to-shoulder
stir-about down in the Plaza
at Villaverde,
at Madrigal de la Vera,

the grainy brew of it
souping up through the night
– then sudden unbearable day
as Julio lifts the lid

and his fingers linger
in what boils harmlessly over them.
I want to ask,
Do the bees never sting him?

But he strolls through the streets
amongst them, the hum
of his Spanish syllables
singing (so one of you

kindly interprets)
of venom and how the bees
inject it of course
to keep the sweet wound sterile.

Thursday

Thursday is Jueves, the day
when the water is due.
Castor has it on Monday,
Pedro on Tuesday, Félix on Wednesday,
then on Thursday...

they'll give us a whole day
of the mountain's water –
like a weekend for two in Paris
or drinks on the house
or, though it leaves us again
and again at midnight, the gift
of suddenly knowing:

how, at the top of the woods,
at a casual undamming,
a boulder of water will rise
from the stream-bed and fall
over and over, any-
where, down into any
aching throat of your land
you happen to choose, green

will spread like a blush each
side of the ditches you've drawn
between fig-trees, the wrinkled
cheeks of your plums will fatten
like children's, your poplars
will ripple Arroyo, arroyo
and throw back their leaves, and even
the dust in the veins of this
poem may turn – mañana, mañana,
Jueves mañana – into mud.

Standees

Goya in the morning:
two leisurely hours in the Prado
while petrol-fumes dance in the streets
and Iberia's
next flight to London practises thunder.

Room after room
of dolled-up royals standing there for him.
'Is that all?' you think, and it is: various
courtly persons
curiously lively or shrewd or unhealthy-looking.

Till this last ghastly yellow
when Madrid falls and we cluster round
and a citizen throws up his arms
in the spurted
glare of musketry on the 3rd of May.

'Ladies and gentlemen...
Señores y Señoras...' The captain
brings us down over London, where a fat
yellow bus
carries, apparently, thirty seated passengers

plus twenty-seven standees,
who, faces burning, sway to its lurch,
lurch to the music of gear-changes,
one arm raised
to the ceiling, the top edge of the frame.

Pylons

Like parents
to you, these first kindly skeletons
on stilts
standing about in your paintings; a power-
station comes

next, then oil-drums,
then in the distance whatever it is
that lilts
away across country from us to you,
from pylon

to pylon.
The same picture but different;
and the same volts
whistling over our heads as those which
in this abstract

of yours, conduct
such a fury of stillness that the old
outline melts
back into canvas under your paint's
turbulence.

53

53 he made, giving North Oxford
such a confident start
in their match against Witney Mills
they never looked back, the paper says.

How the Mills medium-pacers
must have stamped and snorted that
Saturday afternoon of the 1930s,
while he and another academic

slid to 100 together
without risk or frolic or fall
of anything other than numbers
clattering down decade by decade

from the scoreboard. Common
or garden bowling got nowhere
against their neat deflections, their
placements wide of mid-on, and those

mild-mannered defensive strokes
sending even the straightest bowling –
straight from the bunch of the shoulder –
past point, past cover-point.

They clapped of course the wristy
single to leg my father jog-
trotted to reach his 50;
they clapped when they got him out –

as, at public readings, I clap
their lines' robustness – bumping in
past the ears, brushing the heart –
28 of them, 44, never 53.

Engraver's Son Drowned

On June 10th 1825
in the Mill Pond in Angley Wood,
Thomas Jackson Chapman,
beloved son of the celebrated
engraver, aged twelve.

The same age as my son
when the same horror –
in the eyes, in the arms' flounder –
sank him and saved him
in a swimming-pool in France.

He's painting pictures now,
as Tom Chapman, his father's son,
might have been ten years later
if only…Fathers
and fathers of the nearly drowned,

seeing this gravestone,
must have thought, There
but for the grace go I
or goes my son, head-first
arching into the mill-pond,

into the thick
of its wood-juice and soft
self-destructing branches. Sleeves rolled,
good practical daylight reaches in,
offers a helping hand.

Down here, though, we crouch
in the heady throb of our art,
feeding the wheel, letting the wheel
tug and pluck
the weight of us inwards.

Round Robin

Dear friends of Frank, Peta, Mike, Robin,
Jane and Amanda, greetings and our news.
This Christmas we've been almost too busy
to write our usual letter – the level
of Stockitt activity goes up and up!
It's good to keep in touch, though, once a year.

Mike first, of course. There's so much of Mike's news
it won't all fit into a mere Round Robin.
Golf, squash, and tennis he's played over the year
– all three at first-team College level!
The College Ale Society keeps him busy
(he founded it soon after he went up);

he's also written several poems this year
(his aim is now to push his standard up
to National Competition level
before he finishes next year). Robin
won't be home till Christmas Eve. The news
from South Bank Poly is that he's busy

with his Programming etc. The level
of work is not significantly up
on Sixth Form work apparently. No news
is good news if it comes from Robin!
Meanwhile Jane finds that she's less busy
in the Sixth Form than she was last year.

Of course Amanda isn't doing O Level
– Jane passed nine subjects (slightly up
on Mike's achievement, three more than Robin).
Amanda, taking GCSE instead, is busy
riding when not editing the Fifth Year
Weekly Chronicle. Giving Amanda's news

is like it used to be giving Mike's news!
Now Frank. He goes from strength to strength. This year
he's been so busy – the doctor says too busy.
He flies to Rome each week for top-level
meetings, comes back late, next morning gets up
early – and so the family Round Robin

is up to Peta, who's busy – at her level –
but sends you Frank, Amanda, Jane, Robin
and Mike's best wishes for a newsy year.

Four Seasons

Now they've taken everything, you said,
camera, cassette-player, films, tapes, money.
At night you keep a knife beside your bed.

Love, we're horrified. All winter we've read
your letters and worried about security.
Now they've taken everything, you said

– including that Vivaldi you recorded
tape-to-tape at home last summer for me?
At night you keep a knife beside your bed.

What a year you're having: back here my head
sings with your music's verve and energy.
Now they've taken everything, you said.

Autumn in Africa then, red leaves grounded,
the fall. Strange to think that out there somebody –
at night you keep a knife beside your bed –

stoops and switches on and hears, instead
of envy, this clear spring called Vivaldi.
Now they've taken everything, you said.
At night you keep a knife beside your bed.

Villanelle for Elinor

Perhaps a villanelle will do the trick
for me, if not for you in Africa,
crossing the border into Mozambique.

Love, you know it's a war-zone? Every week
we hear of raids and casualties out there.
Perhaps a villanelle will do the trick.

Of course you had to go, you had to take
the path across the mountains. Dear daughter,
crossing the border into Mozambique,

your boots too tight for you, your old ruck-sack
on its last knees, you said in your letter,
perhaps a villanelle will do the trick.

What ease we wrapped you in for you to break
from it so vibrantly: courting danger,
crossing the border into Mozambique,

you stretch yourself, and me on such a rack,
O activist, parental pace-maker,
perhaps a villanelle will do the trick.
Crossing the border into Mozambique.

Scribble

Scribble – flicker of up-strokes, down-strokes;
V-signs, inverted V-signs – is what
the electroencephalograph made
in 1946 of the brainwaves
of a typical Oxford family.
Helmeted, plugged in, we thought
our thoughts: the pencil scribbled
helplessly. I wish I'd kept mine now,
and my father's and mother's –

as I've kept from ten years earlier
this other more than memento,
a drawing by Muirhead Bone
of the Canterbury Quad, St John's.
Eighteen, no, nineteen of the Fellows
are standing about in the shadows
waiting to dine. Outside these walls
there's war, not war, already
war of course. My father, gowned
like the rest of them, hands in pockets,
trousers like half-used toothpaste-tubes,
wouldn't ever, would, then didn't
send us to America. If
it should come to it, he's fit,
not fitted, isn't fit to fight. Fires
anyway. At Nottingham Bradman
has made a double century.
Any moment now the bell will go.
Siren. Bell. Some are hooded for it.
The artist sits at a window.
Against the grey the gowns and hoods
are black. His pencil, he, his pencil
scribble them. Helplessly, with care.

Bricklayer

Bill Cooper, whose eighteen-inch
battlemented brick parapet
I mow my grass – his grass, his
flaking brick-dust – up against,

did everything: went aged sixteen
with fixed bayonet over the top
in France; came back a veteran;
did two years' boyhood in England;
fought again; fought again
twenty years later. In the rich
meantime, married; laid these bricks;
would brick you all you wanted
for sieges – walls, counter-walls, turrets,
arrow-holes even; was champion
local boxer and footballer,
part-time constable; bought, so they say
(he never wrote anything down),
half a pond for five pounds, sailed
muscovies on it, one of which,
ancient, crotchety Charlie, came –
fouled-up wall-perch included –
with the property.

    We're keeping things
much the same: keeping
war going, for instance, and honour
for men of action. I kneel,
bolster and mallet in hand,
to knock Bill Cooper's bricks out
– for use as hard core, to park
cars or write poetry on.

In the Back
('Had he his hurts before?')

Hurts lately grown honourable:
ridiculous, Old Siward's first
terrified thought when, flushed with goodness,
they told him his son was gone –
dead at the hand of the tyrant.
The boy could still be God's soldier
so long as the wounds... The wounds
weren't in the back, were they?

This wound is in the back.
We see the boy running, then,
inside his shirt, this mudball
erupting as the rifle's patience
cracks. Natural as tears the politics
of shootings: youthfulness, innocence,
the back-wound, and the broken English
of the dead Palestinian's father.

They need us there as witnesses.
There where they draw the sheet back,
behind the frail partition, the whole
world noses in and sees dark hair,
the hardly stiffened neck, and a hole
next to the spine. Yes, he'll serve:
look how the shoulders bare their blades
through the thin shirt of the skin.

Near Tunbridge Wells

Watched 'Cry Freedom' again last night:
the Crossroads rioting, Biko's death, Sharpeville etc
depicted
as harshly as ever of course
but different now that Mandela is free.

Re-winding was different too: to see
bullets back in their rifles, a massacre
retracted
as though it could somehow be –
as though yesterday never happened

at a Belfast stadium where, sound
switched to a murmur, the cameras
inspected
the broken flesh of rioting
football fans. It could have been Devon

for colour, red weeping from sandstone;
for tears, it could have been any
impacted
rockface or manface in Britain.
This morning the mind's eye's full of it:

winding, re-winding, the place I inhabit
is Capetown and Belfast, merely the world
contracted.
Here chair-leg and cricket-bat handle
are each a policeman's baton.

Hitching Westward, 1950

Crazy amazing educational
school said, See, before dying,
Stanley Spencer's wall-paintings
in a chapel near Newbury. We saw
soldiers, fleshy unsoldierly
First World War soldiers, painting
each other's flesh wounds (one
purpling another's purple patch
in the side), bathing swollen
legs in a mountain stream
while an officer holding a map
plots their next move, crowding

(in *Resurrection: Macedonia*)

mildly towards us, faces
pressed to the bobbing network
of crosses they each of them bear.
We hitched home before dying,
along A339, lunch tins empty,
past where we had our picnic, past
turnings to Aldermaston – turns
to the left become turns to the right
overlunch –, past where the fence
round the Missile Base would be
in the 1980s, down the Great West Road,
legs heavy, fingers all thumbs.

The Sensible Thing

A sudden storm at lunch-time,
and the Battle of Crécy,
the end of another
crazy spectacular epoch –
its castles, its heads in the clouds –
is postponed for an hour.

My English archers
do the sensible thing:
unfix bow-strings, then stand,
though not at ease, their stuffed
waterproof caps bulging
like apple-pies on their heads.

Their fire-power wins this war.
It's only logical.
The cavalry charge, and the archers
raze every live thing
to the ground the hooves again
and again come drumming on.

When the rain stops,
I go through my inspection.
Doffing caps, cracking jokes about head-lice,
they don't need spurring on
or wishing luck in the battle.
Archers don't need luck.

Like a blind man with his sons,
I ruffle their hair: warm
and wiry as bird's-nests
the heads where the bow-strings were.
'Little Boy', I murmur, 'Fat Man',
or whatever's affectionate.

Noises Off

A fraction of sky falling in,
miles over my head. Unless
it's coal in the stove downstairs
inching closer over the fire of itself,
settling down to be burnt.

It's guns waking me up:
deep in the woods minutely
thundering off at pigeons or rabbits.
Eight hours, ten hours it must be,
perhaps twenty conscious thoughts,

since last night on TV
some expert said they could now
make lightning; not just likenesses
he showed us, but whatever it is
that signals frantically that thunder's coming.

Sunday morning, of course: so quiet
in between the explosions
you might hear the shot animal cry.
Simply count the seconds and say
how far off the explosion is.

Our Master's Voice

We must have caught the crackling somewhere
along Belbroughton; or where Banbury
turns into Bardwell if, late as usual,
we went in bare-faced, through the main gates.

Heads down – we might have been blindfold –
we'd be just about bicycling into
whatever had ghosted coldly up
from the Cherwell during the night,

just about passing the blackened ring
where one of our Lancasters fell
one Sunday afternoon on a placid
North Oxford house, when through the mist

the voice came to us, talking us in
from our childhoods, our Summertown
gardens where the heat of the sun
met the heat off the sunlit brickwork.

Star-jumps they were doing, and we
leaned our bikes on the Maths hut and jumped
like stars, then changed with the rest
to slow, hands-on-hips trunk-rolling.

Clockwise from nine am we rolled,
while the corky trunk of the man
in the playground-pulpit rolled anti-
clockwise – us he was in a mirror,

making men of us, slowly coiling
the thin strings of our back-muscles
(he had rope – we'd seen it – coiled
in the bursting bags on his calves).

Some last days – of a term, of a whole
boyhood – he'd be his crackling self,
except that we for once were to keep
our wits about us and obey him

only when he was O'Grady. 'Arms
raise', he'd snap. Arms twitching to obey,
we'd stand there waiting for 'O'Grady
says "Arms raise"'. Then we'd raise arms,

jump like stars in opposition, leave school,
march, vote against Suez, the Falklands War,
the Bomb, bombing Ghadafi, Star Wars,
Public Schools, Prep Schools, and Belbroughton Road.

To a Poetry Editor

Every Sunday in term-time at four pm
young men would come, like lambs –
little marching lambs on their college ties
with flags over their shoulders –
to the slaughter: suited, blazered,
up from Marlborough, Merchant Taylor's,
Haileybury – though, even in the 1940s,
the drawing-room held its breath
when one young man, under fire
from my mother, admitted to Eton.

The Dean and family at home:
three children somewhere there, not knowing
what they were thinking; their father,
his Yorkshire vowels still, like his eyebrows,
bristling after fifteen years down South;
his wife, clear-eyed anti-élitist,
daughter of Oxford, Oxford mother
extraordinary, moving graciously
amongst young men, pouring them tea
like mild unanswerable questions.

In summer no one was safe,
not even when tea was over. Quoits
in the garden: a rubber ring and a net,
a parapet rather, chest high, the height
of my eyes. My brother crushed the ring
in his hands and watched it wobbling
back into shape as it fell; I
flung at the young men's throats, dared them,
down the gleaming guns of my eyes,
to take this next untakable one.

Scholars, schoolboy heroes, Blues, a Welsh
International once – I can feel
the shine in my eyes as we shook hands
after I'd lost. One's a judge now,
there are public school headmasters,
editors, dons – still holding court,
the other side of the net, at Eton,
at Oxford. I'd fling the ring now,
only I wonder, Is there any chance
of you taking this untakable one?

Rhubarb

Like young beans in July – runners rather than dwarfs –
this early rhubarb snaps into bits in your fingers,
all shin-bone and thigh-bone its pale hockey-stick legs.

Yet not so much legs as curious pink antennae
that somebody's done so well, through the winter months,
to stretch – the sky's the limit – through peat or straw

in a bottomless upturned bucket, that now, poor loves,
they're going for 65p a pound, the scholarship set,
fast-forwarded to Blundell's, Ampleforth, Eton.

Parking

Parking was public outside the College wall.
Entrances had to be clear, but otherwise
anywhere under the trees from the tradesmen's gate
past the drive to the President's Lodgings to the point
where, at skidmarks and scatter of glass, it's
Woodstock or Banbury, where the road to the North divides,
you could drive in south from the Birmingham area
or on the old route from Yorkshire via Rugby
and park, free, head-on to the College, at one point
head-on to an old gatekeeper's cottage
where my father held almost public tutorials.

Narrow barred windows, a small palisade outside.
Inside, he's bathed in the light of his teaching,
the light on the book, the hands holding the book,
the faces flooding over. On the ceiling traffic
spiders about, sometimes turns in full-beam. Too
often, though, he'd be standing dark at the window,
jaw thrust, eyebrows bristling at what most
enraged him, careless parking of cars. A place
reserved for a Fellow casually taken, one
wheel on the pavement even, and my father
would be out there, at his curious rigid worst.

Then, scattering traffic, he'd come striding home,
lyrical now about a lovely Radleian
or lovely Wykehamist whom my mother
really must invite to Sunday tea. Standing
behind her, watching her pencil re-dotting i's,
re-crossing t's, going over and over
this new name on her list, I bristle
with suspicion not at my father calling
this quick-thinking, questioning student of his
lovely – lovely himself for that: it's just
I suspect he kept a place for the boy.

Count Guryev Speaks

(from a portrait by Ingres)

You think I tower.
But I have to tell you
it is perfectly proper

for the human head
held upright
not in absolute spinelessness

to soar above
diminutive white villas
on a sultry plain.

Nor is the scarlet gown
clinging to the long
slope of my shoulder

mere affectation.
We can all attain to it.
We can all speak with my voice.

Oh I know
there's another storm brewing
over the hills behind me.

Storms brew: sometimes
the green evening rages
most handsomely.

Serving Out

Quite silly sometimes
in the early days before Father's trees
had thickened enough to screen
the girls playing tennis
from the eyes of the men in the mill,

Laetitia Wakely served
out of court and over the chicken-wire
Father had rigged against just such
looseness – his girls shouldn't lack,
but they shouldn't waste either –

and into the river beyond,
where, just down from Todmorden,
the Calder mob took over.
What, work fifty-eight hours for the man
in the whirring dark, and then

not come lurching down across boulders
to knock the smile off his face?
And when the bobbing grin of it
still wouldn't sink, not boot it
down-river towards Halifax?

The garden's the sad thing now:
Tom Wakely's old tennis-court
clambering over its netting,
and the summer-house Gibson knocked up
broken-browed, frowning, a V-sign.

As for the man, let's hope
he went too – not mobbed, though,
or furtively, in the early hours,
over the blur of the foot-bridge,
but out through his own front door,

where the black canal lies waiting
for just such prosperous men.
Broad-backed, indifferent,
on shoulders of water it takes them
down, lock by lock, decently.